Kids Running ☺

Have Fun, Get Faster & Go Farther

Carol Goodrow

BREAKAWAY BOOKS
HALCOTTSVILLE, NEW YORK
2008

Kids Running: Have Fun, Get Faster & Go Farther
Copyright © 2008 by Carol Goodrow

ISBN: 978-1-891369-76-6
Library of Congress Control Number: 2007940969
Printed in China

Published by Breakaway Books
P. O. Box 24
Halcottsville, NY 12438
www.breakawaybooks.com

FIRST PRINTING

TABLE OF CONTENTS

THANKING EVERYONE

It's always fun for me to write an acknowledgment page.
It's the page on which
I get to thank the
people who helped
me write my book.

I made a list in my
journal and here it is.

1. Nancy Eldert, a long lost college
friend, for her encouragement.

2. Kevin Bouley, one of my Happy Feet Club sponsors, who
enabled me to provide my TREASURE chapter book for the
kids in my club.

3. Mark Summers, my original Happy Feet Club sponsor.

4. My husband, Kevin, for helping me with the jokes.

5. Bev Vaida, for proofreading and praising my work.

6. My family, Keith, Josie, Ted, Alex, Brianne, Lois, & June.

7. Amby Burfoot, for his helpful suggestions and positive
support.

8. Garth Battista, for publishing my books.

9. Linda Rallo, for reading my rough manuscript to her class
and ALL my teacher friends whom I work with day in and
day out.

10. Last but not least, Coach Ed Poirier, for his many
contributions to the book and for his daily help with the
kidsrunning.com Web site.

Running can be a fun, feel-good activity if you treat it right. So come along with us as we get ready to run.

Are you wearing a good pair of sneakers? They don't have to be expensive running shoes, but they need flexible soles, heels, and toes.

Do they fit and are they comfortable? Running sneakers must fit just right so they feel comfy and snug.

Are they tied? If you can't tie, then learn. You will get the most secure fit by tying your shoes with laces. You might also try elastic curly laces. These laces can be pulled snug, and they don't need to be tied. But no matter how you secure your shoes to your feet, be it Velcro or any new elastic type closing, running sneakers must have a snug fit to prevent accidents and injuries.

Practice   *Learn*

Not too loose.

Not too tight.

Tie them so they fit just right.

AT THE RUNNING STORE

Take a trip to a running store. You can have a shoe expert look at your feet to tell you if you have high arches, medium arches, or low arches. They might recommend a certain type of shoe to match your foot.

Low Arches = Motion Control or Stability Shoe
Medium Arches = Stability Shoe or Cushioned Shoe
High Arches = Cushioned Shoe

When you try on your shoes, walk a little and go for a short jog. Some stores have running tracks right in the store! That makes it even more fun to go shoe shopping. Make sure that your shoes have a snug fit. They will feel more comfortable as you break them in.

AT HOME

1. Analyze your footprints. Soak your feet and walk on a sidewalk. Do your prints show a low, medium, or high arch?

2. Compare your walking and running footprints. How do your prints differ when you walk and when you run? Mark off a distance and go for a run. Count your footprints. Then walk the same distance. Count your footprints. How do the number of walking and running footprints compare?

 Running shoes are made for all types of feet.

Low Arches   Medium Arches   High Arches

CHITCHAT

My blue shoes make running a breeze.

My black shoes make me run like the wind.

CASSANDRA: I have two pairs of running sneakers.

ALEX: I have one pair of good sneakers and one pair of REAL running shoes that I got at the running store.

CASSANDRA: My shoes are bouncy.

ALEX: I can tell! My real running shoes are reflective. They glow in the dark.

CASSANDRA: Sweet! I like to wear my rainbow laces.

ALEX: Red laces bring me good luck.

CASSANDRA: I wrote, "Love to run," on a pair of laces.

ALEX: I wrote, "Catch me if you can," on a pair of mine.

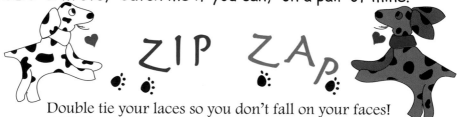

ZIP ZAP

Double tie your laces so you don't fall on your faces!

Which color laces do you prefer?

You like reds.
I like blues.
Runners love their comfy shoes.

What would you write on your laces?

THE SEASONS: SUMMER, FALL, WINTER, SPRING

Runners dress according to the seasons and different weather conditions.

SUMMER
Shorts, thin T-shirt or singlet, shoes, and socks. A cap is optional. If you're out in the bright sun, use sunscreen.

FALL
The weather varies. Start adding layers when it gets cooler. Long sleeve shirt, long pants, gloves, and hats are all layers you can put on over your shorts and tees. You can take them off if you get too hot while running.

WINTER
As it gets colder add sweatshirts, sweaters, fleece vests, and thin jackets. Put mittens on over your gloves. Wear a wool knit hat. Check the treads on your sneakers. You will need deep ones. There may be patches of snow or ice that can be slippery. Good treaded soles will help keep you on your feet.

SPRING
As it warms up, start shedding your layers. Make sure that you have a light rain resistant jacket so you can enjoy a run in a spring shower. If it's cool, change into dry clothing as soon as you get home.

When you run your kinetic energy increases.
It makes you feel warmer.

When you get too hot,
simply take off a layer.
When you get cold again,
just put it back on.

Sneaker Vocabulary

A general sports shoe and a
running shoe should have these parts.

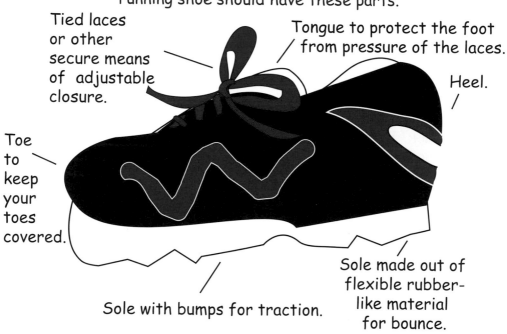

Tied laces or other secure means of adjustable closure.

Tongue to protect the foot from pressure of the laces.

Heel.

Toe to keep your toes covered.

Sole with bumps for traction.

Sole made out of flexible rubber-like material for bounce.

Wear shoes in good repair.

Heel, toe,
Heel, toe,
Around the track, two laps to go.

SPIKES: From Coach Ed

Spikes are running shoes with metal points on the soles. They are worn by experienced competitors.

For runners 8 and under, spikes may actually get in the way and hinder performance. Many times a young runner may stumble from the spike gripping the track the wrong way.

If you are 9 years or over and run with proper form then you may want to use spikes for sprint competitions.

When some athletes lace up their spikes they mentally feel like they are ready to race. They are thinking: This is not practice, this is not a game, this is a race and I am ready.

A few cautions when using a spike running shoe.
• Never use a spike longer than the recommended size for the track. Track surfaces are not all alike. A meet director will usually post the recommended maximum spike length for a particular track. A longer spike will not grip properly and could even damage the track surface.
• In cross country meets athletes are forced to run on asphalt or cement surfaces in addition to dirt or grass. An athlete could easily slip and fall in a race with a spike on. You and your coach will need to determine if using a spike is worth the risk.
• A spiked shoe must fit very snugly, almost like a glove. For that reason wearing spikes may become expensive because a child can grow a few shoe sizes in a short time.

My final thought on spikes for youth runners is you don't need them unless you are at the highest level of youth competition and hundredths of a second will determine the outcome of the race.

Ed Poirier is a Youth Wellness Specialist with the Attleboro YMCA.

Wear socks. Runners wear wicking socks. Wicking socks keep your feet dry. They can be made of wool or a high tech fabric like polyester. Cyclists wear cool socks with stripes, smilies, sharks, flowers, cats, ice cream cones, or dragons. You can wear cycling socks to run in, too.

Break in new sneakers by walking and running in them before wearing them to a race, fun run, or to school. You'll feel better in your shoes and you'll prevent blisters.

If you don't wear sneakers or running shoes to school, pack a pair in your backpack for recess. Recess is a great time to exercise large muscles by running.

Activities
Write about your laces.
Create your own mottoes.
Draw your dream sneakers.
Design some cool socks.

How do your
shoes fit?

CLOTHING

While you're at the running store, take a look at the clothing department. You'll find:

Wicking Socks - Remember, wicking socks are the wool or high tech socks that runners wear. These socks absorb the sweat away from your body and help prevent blisters. Kids may do fine with cotton socks because they don't sweat as much as adults. But if you get blisters and you are starting to sweat, then it's time to start wearing wicking socks.

Wicking Shirts and Shorts - You can also find tees and shorts in wicking materials. Cotton tees are fine for kids but as you grow older and sweat more, you will want to start looking for clothing that also wicks the sweat away from your body.

ACCESSORIES

Hats
Baseball type caps keep the sun off your face. Knit caps are for cold weather.

Heat escapes through your extremities (head, feet, & hands).

Gloves & Mittens
Gloves work as a first layer on a cool day. Nice roomy mittens go over gloves on a very cold day.

Sometimes you'll see runners wearing hats and gloves with shorts and tees. They are staying warm by protecting their extremities.

CARDIO BASICS

Cardio is exercise that makes your heart and lungs stronger. Running, cycling, brisk walking, swimming, and dancing are all types of cardio.

When you run, you breathe faster and more deeply. This helps your lungs get stronger and helps you get more air into your lungs. More air means more oxygen.

If you exercise, your heart beats faster and gets stronger. It has to hurry up to move your blood throughout your body. Your blood is carrying oxygen to your body's cells.

And when your heart and lungs are stronger you can exercise more easily!

Blood carries oxygen and nutrients.

Your lungs help you breathe and talk.

My heart gets stronger,

With each step.

Running gives me lots of pep.

INCREASING YOUR CARDIO FITNESS

You can increase your cardiovascular fitness by exercising longer and harder, but you need to do this gradually. **You should be able to talk while you walk or jog.** Over time you will be able to exercise with more intensity.

Another way that you can measure and monitor your exercise is to keep track of your heart rate. Many athletes train with heart rate monitors. A heart rate monitor is an instrument that measures how many times a minute your heart beats. You can also find your heart rate by taking your pulse. Place two fingers on the carotid artery on your neck and count how many beats you feel in a minute.

You can find your maximum heart rate by **subracting your age from 220.** If you are 10 years old, your maximum heart rate would be 220 - 10 = 210. If you **multiply your maximum heart rate by .70 (or find 70% of your maximum heart rate),** you can find out the approximate rate you should work at to increase your cardio fitness. 210 X .70 = 147. This is your target rate.

220 - Your Age = Max. Heart Rate

Max. Heart Rate X .70 = Target Rate

Use a calculator.
Punch in 220. Subtract your age.
Multiply by .70.
The answer is your Target Heart Rate.

CASSANDRA: Remember when I used to gasp for breath?

ALEX: Your heart and lungs weren't strong enough to run far.

CASSANDRA: Now I can!

ALEX: All the way to the park whenever you want.

CASSANDRA: I can even run a mile, IF I pace myself.

ALEX: Someday you'll run a 5-K and I'll do a marathon - someday.

Q: How did the healthy heart get to the Olympics?
A: It kept on beating!

Start out easy.
Pick up the pace.
Earn a medal at the Chipmunk Chase.

Q: How is a healthy heart like a wind-up clock?
A: They both keep ticking.

JUMPING ROPE

Another form of cardio is jumping or skipping rope.

Jumping rope has many of the benefits of running. It is good for your heart, allows your lungs to take in added oxygen, helps you with coordination, and it can be done to a beat.

The **beat or rhythm** of jumping rope makes it fun, but even though it is fun, it takes concentration or **it's easy to misstep**.

So, for as long as children have had jump ropes, they've had fun with snappy "jump-'til-you-miss" jump-rope jingles. These jingles may include counting up or down, brainstorming words, days of the week, months of the year, and more. You may already have a favorite jump-rope jingle.

And you can use them with other physical activities: jogging in place, bouncing balls, and jumping jacks.

COUNTING BY 2s
Charlie Cheetah is at the track.
He wants to run in a potato sack.
He runs two laps, and then runs four.
He runs 6 laps, and the crowd yells, "More!"
How many laps did Charlie run?
2, 4, 6...

Running, cycling, walking, and swimming are some of the best cardio exercises.

Cardio - a. Exercise that makes the heart beat faster. b. A prefix meaning "of the heart."

Contract - To become shorter and tighter.

Heart - Muscular organ that pumps blood through your body.

Lungs - Organs in our bodies that work to remove carbon dioxide from the blood and get oxygen to our blood.

Muscle - Part of the body that can contract to produce movement.

Organ - Part of the body that has a job to do.

Put your heart into your exercise.

Run and pedal.
Skip and jump.
Make your heart work like a pump.

CARDIO: From Coach Ed

CARDIO WORKOUTS
Jogging, cycling, rowing a boat, and brisk walking are powerful cardio workouts. These are all activities that you can do for long periods of time. Jumping rope and dancing are favorites because they involve rhythm. Some children can dance and jump rope for an hour!

BENEFIT TO RUNNING
As your lungs and heart get stronger from cardio workouts, you will be able to run faster for a longer distance. In training for running you will need to have a good mix of cardio training for your heart and lungs and strength training for your leg muscles.

A combination of short fast running and long slower running will give you the balance that you need to be a better athlete. Here is a wonderful secret about cardio. You can call it exercise but it is really just playing!

COUNTING BY 100s
Jenny Jacobs is at the meet.
She runs like a centipede with 100 feet.
She runs so fast, doesn't want to be last.
She runs 1000 meters and then gets passed.
How many meters did Jenny run?
100, 200...

Ed Poirier is a Youth Wellness Specialist with the Attleboro YMCA.

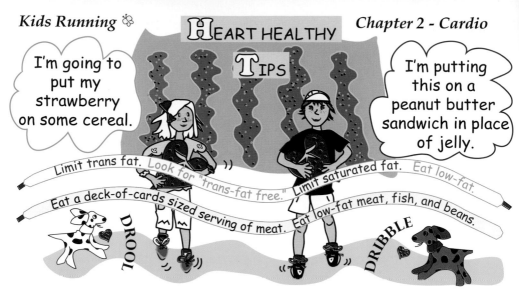

Good runners prefer heart-healthy foods with lots of vitamins, minerals, and fiber. You can too. Choose:

FRUITS AND VEGETABLES - Eat lots of these for snacks and with your meals. They should be the base of your diet.

WHOLE-GRAINS - Look for the word "whole" on your cereals and breads. It should be listed as the first ingredient. Use whole-grain flour when you bake cookies.

HEALTHY FAT - Get your fat from sources such as fish and nuts. Choose olive oil over butter & canola oil over shortening.

THINK LOW-FAT - Protein and dairy should be low in fat.

Activities

Pack a fruit and veggie with your lunch.
Read the nutrition labels on foods.
Bake whole-wheat muffins.
Mix oil and vinegar for salad dressing.
Use sliced fruit instead of jelly in PBJs.

Running gives you a healthy appetite.

Avoid supersized portions.

TAG GAME: From The Happy Feet, Healthy Food Kids' Club

Dogs and Ducks

1. One boy and one girl are "dogs". They stand in the middle of the field barking. They are the taggers or "IT".

2. The rest of the kids are "ducks". They stand on the side of the field quacking.

3. Leader yells, "Go," and all the children run. The ducks try to run to the other side of the field and back without being tagged by a dog. If they are tagged, they join the dogs in the center of the field and are also "IT".

4. Leader waits until all the children have gone across and back and then yells, "Go." Play continues like this until all the ducks turn into dogs.

5. Play and have fun! Arf, arf, arf! Quack, quack, quack!

6 Finish with a slow lap of the field or a nature hike.

COUNTING BY 20s

Andy Andrews went strawberry pickin'.

But he ran a relay with a rubber chicken.

He ran twenty meters, then he ran another twenty.

No berries in his basket – should have been plenty!

How many meters did Andy run? 20, 40...

You can have a lot of fun with both walking and running, so no need to argue.

When you're first starting a running program, a combination of walking AND running is often best. It's a great way to get all of your muscles and organs used to longer periods of exercise.

Some people always walk & run to complete long distance races, others walk & run when they take their dogs outdoors for some exercise. **Combining walking and running is natural.** Watch your friends playing at recess. They run, sprint, and then walk a little.

Walk & run fitness routines and games are great activities for you and your friends to play together even if you have different levels of fitness.

Walk the dog.

Should I walk,
Or should I run?
Both make moving lots of fun.

Run and sprint.

WALKING & RUNNING WITH YOUR DOG

Want to have some fun with your dog? Get the leash and watch your dog romp. Going for a walk & run can overwhelm your pet with happiness.

1. **Walking & running are great for your dog,** but like beginning runners, dogs need time to get used to running longer distances. And hot weather can be tough on all dogs so take walking breaks.

2. **Exercise will make your dog thirsty.** You can buy folding water bowls to carry with you for your dog.

3. **Bring along a plastic bag to scoop up your dog's poop.** If you don't, he may leave some on a neighbor's front yard.

4. **If your dog pulls you along, take your dog to obedience school.** He will learn to walk & run on a leash.

5. Take control. **Teach the words,"Sit, come, heel, stay, leave it."** These words will help you have a successful walk & run with your dog. **"Heel" will tell your dog to move at your pace.** Add the commands, "Slow" and "Fast".

6. **A dog who has exercised is happier and calmer.** Take your dog for a long walk & run early in the morning and you will have a nice cooperative dog for the afternoon. Take him after school and you'll be able to do your homework without distractions.

FAVE SENTENCES

"Want to go for a WALK?"   *"Let's go RUNNING!"*

Our Favorite Words
Come, sit, stay, heel, leave it,
fast, & slow.

CASSANDRA: Gage and Karlie run too fast for me.

ALEX: They are speedy. Let's do the butterfly route.

CASSANDRA: What's that?

ALEX: It's a play-together route in the shape of a butterfly. We all sprint down a center "butterfly lane" and then it's your choice. You turn right to jog around a "butterfly wing" or you turn left to walk around the other "butterfly wing". When you get back to the start you sprint down the center lane again.

CASSANDRA: I'll make paper butterflies for everyone.

ALEX: I'll bring my orange cones to mark the course.

Kids who run and walk together, end up best of friends forever.

Run at your own pace.

You walk fast.
I jog slow.
Around the butterfly wings we go.

Include your friends.

CONDITIONING WORKOUT: From Coach Ed

Here is a useful workout that sprinters and distance runners can do together. Find a neighborhood route that's about 2 miles long. Then repeatedly walk for 2 minutes and run for 20 seconds.

If you are a sprinter, this workout will improve your endurance and you'll have fun while doing it because you'll be running with other kids. **And if you are a distance runner, you'll benefit from it by improving your "kick" for the finish of a distance race.**

These workouts should be done once a week, 52 weeks a year in snow, rain, wind, and hot weather. Seeing you and your friends running in the neighborhood will inspire adults and other kids to get out and have fun.

Mix it up. Try these workouts for 1 - 2 miles.

Walk 2 minutes, run 20 seconds.
Walk 2 minutes, run 20 seconds.

Try it another way, another day.

Walk 3 minutes, run 30 seconds.
Walk 3 minutes, run 30 seconds.

And still another!

Walk 1 minute, run 10 seconds.
Walk 1 minute, run 10 seconds.

Remember, exercise can be done anywhere!

Walking, running, jogging, and sprinting are forms of locomotion. Which is your favorite?

Jog - To run slowly.

Run - To move faster than walking and never have both feet on the ground at the same time.

Sprint - To run very quickly for a short distance.

Walk - To move by foot at a natural pace and never have both feet off the ground at the same time.

Run and play.

Walk to the left.
Jog to the right.
Time to sprint with all your might!

INTERVIEW WITH JEFF GALLOWAY

Jeff Galloway is a former U.S. Olympian who once ran with a famous runner, Steve Prefontaine. He is the founder of the Galloway RUN-WALK method.

When should children walk & run?

Jeff: I've found that when walk breaks are included from the beginning of a run, runners don't feel tired and achy. They go just as fast overall - as if they ran the whole distance. Walk breaks allow people to go farther, feel better, and recover more quickly.

Walk breaks make running more fun. Many kids get discouraged when running continuously. They feel that they weren't made to run. When walk breaks are used in the correct ratio from the beginning (ex. run 9 minutes, walk 1 minute or another repeated pattern), every child can keep increasing distance and feel like a champion.

Can you get faster or go farther with a walk & run?

Jeff: Yes, the average improvement in a 5-K race, among those who used to run continuously, is about 3 minutes.

Is this something that you do?

Jeff: I take walk breaks every minute on just about every run; it's a wonderful way to warm up.

Something to try!

For Parents: Jeff is the author of FIT KIDS, SMARTER KIDS.
jeffgalloway.com/fitkids.html

Be safe. When the weather is hot, walking breaks can help you and your pets exercise longer and more safely. But if it's too hot, take a break from outdoor running. Running can make you feel like it's 20 degrees hotter. Take more care on days when it's in the 80s or 90s.

Make up exercise routes that include walking, running, and sprinting. Use creative shapes and rules. Include other types of locomotion such as skipping, hopping, and leaping. This variety will keep your exercise interesting.

Bring water to drink before, during, and after you play.

Activities
Make up a triangle route.
Have a run, jog, and walk lane.
Then decide what to do at the corners.
Ideas: Sing, jog in place, do jumping
jacks, do crunches, or do push-ups.

Walk and
run.

GETTING STARTED: For the Inactive Beginner

Here is a simple schedule for getting started with exercise. This is a schedule for you if you are a total beginner or have been inactive for a long time. Start out by following the routines. Do more when you feel strong.

M: Walk for 1 min., jog for 10 sec. Repeat for 1/4 mile.

T: Walk for 1 min., jog for 15 sec. Repeat for 1/4 mile.

W: Walk for 30 sec., jog for 15 sec. Repeat for 1/4 mile.

Th: Walk for 30 sec., jog for 15 sec. Repeat for 1/4 mile.

F: Walk for 30 sec., jog for 20 sec. Repeat for 1/4 mile.

S: Walk for 30 sec., jog for 30 sec. Repeat for 1/4 mile.

S: Take a long walk.

COUNT DOWN 10-1
Betsy Beagle is at the zoo.
She's doing 10 laps with a Pekepoo.
They walk one fast and run one slow.
How many more laps do they have to go?
10, 9...

Drinking water before, during, and after exercise will keep your body hydrated.

Eating the proper foods will give you energy to run and will also help restore your body after exercising.

Fruits and vegetables fill your body with vitamins and nutrients. Whole grains and fruits give you a lot of energy.

Proteins like fish, chicken, and meat help you rebuild your muscles.

Healthy fats from fish, nuts, and vegetable oils give you energy, are great for your heart, and good for your brain.

A strawberry for you, a carrot for me,
Bright yellow sun, green trees to see.
Deep blue skies, a violet flower,
Rainbow treasures surround the hour.

                                      www.carolgoodrow.com

BREAKFAST FOR RUNNING KIDS

Having a good breakfast is the best way to jump start your day. Put the fuel in your body first thing in the morning so that you'll be active and ready to play and learn all day.

But what to eat for breakfast? Whole-grain cereal with no- to low-fat milk, a generous portion of fruit, a glass of water, a little juice (optional), and perhaps a piece of whole-grain toast combine to make a low-fat and hearty breakfast, good for your weight and filling, too!

If you can't find the time to breakfast at home, then pack a morning snack for school with fruit and dry whole-grain cereal. Eat it on the school bus or at morning snack. Just don't go all morning without your fuel/food.

Breakfast is fuel for champions.

1. Breakfast helps you focus and may help your memory.

2. Breakfast fuels you for the day.

3. A good breakfast is low-fat, low-sugar, and fills you up.

Alexander's Breakfast
Whole-grain Cereal
No-fat Milk
2 Peaches
Water

ALEX: I have some peapods for a healthy snack and half of a peanut butter peach sandwich for my energy snack.

CASSANDRA: I have a banana for a healthy snack and some whole-grain crackers to give me energy for running.

ALEX: Hey, how do you make a veggie roll?

CASSANDRA: Gee, I don't know.

ALEX: You put it on the top of a slide and give it a little push!

CASSANDRA: And how do you make a veggie dip?

ALEX: You take if for a short swim at the lake.

Food for a healthy diet? Just bake it, don't fry it.

Q: What's red on the outside, white on the inside and goes around in circles?

Sweet and fresh.
Hydrating too.
Oranges are very good for you.

A: An apple on a merry-go-round.

CASSANDRA'S BAKING TIPS for your Just-One Treats

1. Use wooden spoons. They will make your baking experience feel cozy. My favorite one is the one in the bowl. My grandmother gave it to me.

My dog is my best buddy when I bake!

2. Use a few dark-chocolate chocolate chips. A little **dark chocolate is good for you** but don't use too many! Practice **MODERATION** (don't overdo it).

3. Use **whole-grain pastry flour** for your treats. Make sure it says "PASTRY". You can find it in the health-food section.

Whole-grain Pastry Flour

4. **Use less sugar.** The recipe will still taste good.

5. Add some raisins. They are fat-free, with lots of vitamins, minerals and fiber. They have iron. **Girls, in particular, need iron. They are packed with energy for all runners.** Oh, I forgot. Add oatmeal.

6. Don't use shortening. It can be high in trans fat that is bad for you. Even if the recipe calls for shortening, use a healthy oil instead. **Be smart, use canola oil.** If you use butter, use only the tiniest bit in the whole world. It has a lot of saturated fat. Saturated fat is not good for you!

Learn to read the labels on your ingredients.

KITCHEN VOCABULARY

Whoa!

Stop!

Spot's got the chicken!

Freezer: icy compartment packed with fish, seafood, lean beef, lean pork, and lean chicken.

Veggie Bin: drawer with potatoes (sweet or white), broccoli, greens, tomatoes, cukes, & peppers.

No, Spot!

CHOMP

CRUNCH

Fruit Basket: container stuffed with melons, berries, oranges, grapefruit, kiwi, bananas, grapes, & apples.

Cupboard: cabinet chock-full of whole-grain bread, cereal, rice, granola bars, nuts oils, beans, peanut butter, & raisins.

Fridge: cold compartment stocked with low-fat milk, eggs, cheese, low-fat sour cream, & yogurt.

KARLIE'S BREAKFAST - Whole-grain cereal topped with blueberries and low-fat milk.

CASSANDRA'S SNACK - Peapods and low-fat sour cream dip.

ALEXANDER'S LUNCH - Turkey sandwich on whole-grain bread with Romaine lettuce and low-fat cheese. Small apple.

GAGE'S SNACK - Red grapes and whole-grain crackers.

KARLIE'S SUPPER - Trout, salad, brown rice, and whole-grain bread.

ALEXANDER'S SNACK - Baby carrots and hummus.

CASSANDRA'S TREAT - 1/2 cup ice cream with peaches.

Q: Why did the mama carrot not let the baby carrot into the fridge?

Veggie lasagna,
Bound to get some on ya!

A: She didn't want the baby to be fresh!

STAYING LEAN

The energy that you need to keep running comes from food. Food is meant to fuel your body so that you can stay active, do your school work, and have some fun along the way.

The energy that you get from food is called calories. You need these calories to move, and grow. If you are eating too many calories and not balancing your eating with physical activity, you can start to gain too much weight. This is easy to do when you must sit in school and in front of the TV or computer for hours.

It's important to walk, run, and play to help your body balance the energy that comes in (gets eaten) with the energy that goes out (gets used up). Every person's body uses up energy at a different rate.

But here are some things you can do to stay healthy:

1. Balance your eating with exercise.

2. Eat more fruits and vegetables. Limit energy dense foods such as sweets, soda, juice, white bread, and foods made with trans or saturated fat. An energy dense food has a lot of calories for a small portion of food.

3. Eat lean protein.

4. Eat whole grains.

5. Have plenty of fruits and veggies available for snacking.

Fruit for snack helps us fill up. We keep our waists slim and our bodies nourished.

We add whole-grains for snack when we run a lot.

Eat breakfast a couple of hours before a workout. Have whole-grains, protein, and fruit. Try a whole-grain English Muffin, a little peanut butter, and banana slices.

Eat something light right after a workout. Have low-fat dairy and fruit with whole-grains. Try orange slices, a small bagel (or a part of a medium bagel), and a small low-fat yogurt.

Eat a hearty meal within 2-3 hours of your workout. Have protein, vegetables, and whole-grains. Try a portion of chicken, lots of stir-fried veggies made in olive oil, and a whole-grain roll or some brown rice. Fruit makes a nutritious dessert. Add **one** treat if you wish.

Treats are fun, but just eat one.

Activities
Plan an ideal eating day.
What will you have for breakfast?
How about after a fun run?
What is your favorite veggie, fruit, and protein?

Running
uses up
energy.

Food replaces used-up energy.

GAGE'S COOKING TIPS for Kid Athletes

1. If you want to fuel your body, then you have to **have your food ready the day before.** If it's not ready, your mind might say, "Eat something healthy," but your hands might pick up some junk food and before you know it you're filling your body with food fit for a couch potato.

2. **Make a big salad** with lettuce, nuts, and dried fruit. Add some salmon. Put it in baggies so you can grab a mini-salad anytime.

3. **Make baggies of baby carrots. Take them to school.** All the kids like them. They'll want some of yours.

4. **If you are going to be running a lot, take a baggie of trail mix.** Trail mix has so much energy that you could probably run to the moon.

5. **To make great trail mix you need nuts,** granola, dried fruit, and any other little tidbits that you can think of.

Fun runs are just-do-your-best events! They are for every type of runner. You don't have to be fast to enter.

Fun runs vary in distance. If you look around, you can find one with the distance just right for you. You can find fun runs with very short sprint distances of 50 meters, and you can find fun runs that are long distances of 5-Ks.

Fun runs are often free for kids. Many adult races also have a kids' fun run. Sometimes they are free and other times you must pay to enter. When you do pay, the money often is going to a good cause or a charity to help others.

Sometimes you will earn a medal, T-shirt, or ribbon for completing a fun run. Usually all children who enter earn one of these prizes at a fun run. **But children should always leave the event with a feeling of pride for participating.**

The sun warms your face.
The breeze tickles your skin.
Lift your knees.
Let the running begin.

THE FUN RUN

No matter where you live you should be able to find a fun run. If your school has one, then you're all set! But sometimes it's fun to travel to a fun run.

SEARCH
You can start with a Google search. With the help of your parents, use the Internet. Type in "google.com", then type the name of your state and "fun run". You can also search with the words "kids' running event" or "kids' race". You might search for 5-Ks or marathons that also have a kids' fun run.

KIDS' MARATHONS
Some marathons also have a kids' marathon. You sign up early, keep track of your miles, and then do your fun run as part of the marathon event. This way, you run a total of about 26 miles over a long period of time. Sometimes you run 1/4, 1/2, or 1 mile each day.

DAYS

Krissy Kangaroo is at the park,

She's leaping and prancing with her dog named Bark.

She leaps 7 times and what does she say?

"I'm naming the days till my next birthday."

Which days does she name?

Monday, Tuesday...

ALEX: Want to get ready for the fun run?

CASSANDRA: I think I'll jog for 5 minutes without stopping.

ALEX: I'll time myself on the half-mile.

CASSANDRA: But remember, Sprints Charming, the fun run isn't a race. It doesn't matter how fast you go!

ALEX: Maybe not to you, Goldiwalks, but I want to be the first to cross the finish line.

CASSANDRA: And I just want to cross that line and get my medal.

ALEX: I'll be at the finish cheering you on. Take a walking break if you need one. Just be yourself and you'll do fine.

Run, jog, scurry. Dash, dart, hurry. Fast or slow ~ don't worry!

Start out easy, then pick up the pace.

Finish first,
Or finish last.
Either way, have a blast!

Walk if you need to take a break.

CASSANDRA'S PLAN

This is my friend John. He is visually impaired. He reads Braille. Most of the time he uses a cane to walk, but he needs a guide to run. If he doesn't have a guide, he will run into something. That happened one day and that something was a big pole. I know, because I was there.

I like to be his guide. I hold his wrist and we run together.

There's a big Thanksgiving race that John always goes to watch, with his family. He stands there for an hour and listens to the runners go by even on cold rainy days - like last year when I stayed at home under the covers because it was just too freezing. He is very hardy. Some day I am going to be his guide in that race so that we can walk & run it together. That will be so much fun for us.

MONTHS

Squeezy Squirrel & my friend Mary,
Jog in the forest in January.
No matter the month, they're always here,
Running trails like a herd of deer.
Name the months that they run.
January, February...

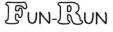

Bib Number - The running number you will wear on the front of your T-shirt during a fun run.

Hydrate - To drink water or other liquids.

Kick - A burst of speed. A spurt of fast running.

Pace - Your rate of running (often slow and steady).

Participate - To take part. To be part of.

Walking break - Walking to take a rest.

Water stop - A table with little cups of water for runners.

Winner - Anyone who crosses the finish line.

Pass me first,
Then I'll pass you.
Move aside,
I'm slipping through!

THE RELAY

The best way to get ready for a fun run is to stay active. Remember, this isn't a race so you don't need to be the speediest, **but once you circle the date on your calendar, you should start your training**. A basic running relay is a fun way to train. You will need a course and two teams. The course needs a start/finish line and a turnaround marker. The 1st runner from each team runs around the turnaround marker and back across, the start line, passes a baton gives a high 5, or yells, "Go!" Then the next player runs.

Runner X
Runner X

Start

Turn-around   Turn-around

You can make this into a fun kids' game by using something creative for the turnaround like a: stuffed monkey, doll, Frisbee, tree, rubber duck, flower garden, or an old hat. **The more FUN, the better!**

COUNTING BY 5s

Ollie Owl is on the road.
He has a net to catch some toads.
He catches 5 and then catches 10.
He catches 5 more and then he's hungry again!
How many toads does Ollie catch?
5, 10, 15...

Riddle: I shine like a star and am round like the sun. I belong to children who have run.

Tips

Answer: A fun run medal, of course!

Sign up!! Run your own pace. Be a winner - finish! Treasure your memories.

Some fun runs allow dogs. Don't bring your dog unless they do. Follow the rules.

Something's making me hungry!

My medal looks good enough to eat!

Signing up for a fun run gives you something to look forward to. Mark your calendar. Tell your friends and family.

Train by exercising every day. Run, walk, and play. Set goals. If you can run 5 minutes without stopping, then set your goal for 6 minutes. Practice until you reach your goal.

Learn to pace yourself. Start out easy. Run steady. Go faster when you feel strong.

If you like to sprint, go for it. Sprint short distances, then jog a little, then sprint again. Take walking breaks if you need them.

Running gives you memories to treasure.

Activities
Sign up for a fun run.
Make a training plan.
Write down your fun run goals.
Go out for a little run to celebrate.

Fun runs
are festivals
of fitness.

ALEXANDER'S END-OF-THE-FUN-RUN REPORT

1. I was about 10 meters from the finish line when I started to sprint. I ran as fast as the wind. I passed 4 runners. People on the sidelines were yelling, "KICK! Look at that fast guy go!"

2. When I crossed the finish line, I did a high five with the one kid who beat me. I turned around and gave a thumbs up sign to one of the runners I passed. Then he shook my hand.

3. I put my medal on right away so that I wouldn't lose it.

4. I remembered to say, "Thank you," for my medal and goody bag even though I was tired.

5. I drank water, then went to look for some food.

6. I went back to the finish line to see my friends finish. Karlie was there waiting, too. I wanted to cheer them on.

7. We walked & jogged a little so that we wouldn't be sore the next day. We were removing lactic acid from our bodies by moving around.

8. I found a pen in my goody bag. I wrote some information on the back of my running number: race name, place (2nd kid), time, and weather.

9. I looked to make sure all of the food in my goody bag was wrapped because of the next thing I did. See number ten.

10. I took off my shoes and socks and put them in my goody bag. I put on my sports sandals that I had left by my bike. I wiggled my toes. AAAH!

Make this fun run be the first of many to come.

CROSS-TRAINING BASICS

Runners often cross-train. When you cross-train you participate in other sports to help your running and fitness.

Cycling is fun and it is good for you. It's a great cardio work-out and it helps strengthen your leg muscles. When you cycle you give your body a rest from running because you are working your muscles in a different way.

Swimming is another popular activity. It's good for your lungs and heart. Swimming is non-impact. When you swim, you give your legs and feet a break from pounding on the earth.

Many sports are good for cross-training: hiking, skate-boarding, dancing, horseback riding, skiing, and kayaking are all types of cross-training.

Q: What's pink, has 2 wheels, and rattles? A: A piggy bank riding a bike.

cycle   Like a tree-trunk-climbing monkey, ʀide
And a gallavanting hound,
You can use your bike to wander,
Up and down the hilly ground.

YOUTH TRIATHLONS: From Coach Ed

Triathlon, 3 events, one right after the other. If you can swim, ride a bicycle, and run, you might enjoy doing a triathlon. There are many youth triathlons around the country and training for one can get you in great athletic shape with an all-around workout.

Swimming will give you a full-body, non-impact workout. Riding a bike will help you with fast leg movements and balance. Running uses your legs and lower body. All three events build up your heart and lungs.

A typical youth triathlon might consist of a 100-meter swim (4 lengths of a pool), 4-mile bike ride, and 1-mile run.

If you are going to give a triathlon a try, remember to train for a longer distance than you will swim in the tri. If you have a 100-meter swim to complete, train to swim 200 meters. That way you will be confident in the water. The same with the bike and run. If the bike portion of the race is 4 miles, train to ride 5 miles fast. If the triathlon run is 1 mile, train to run 1.5 miles.

	Your First Triathlon				
Swim (train) (race)		Cycle (train) (race)		Run (train) (race)	
200 m	100 m	5 mi.	4 mi.	1.5 mi.	1 mi.
	Competitive Triathlon				
Swim (train) (race)		Cycle (train) (race)		Run (train) (race)	
200 m	100 m	4 mi.	2 mi.	2 mi.	1 mi.

Competitive athletes should be training for at least double the required distance for each event in the race.

Imagine getting all your friends together on one day to go for a swim, then to ride your bikes, and after that to run around the neighborhood or playground for a while. That is a triathlon. Is it an athletic event or just plain fun?

Ed Poirier is a Youth Wellness Specialist with the Attleboro YMCA.

ALEX: Karlie can't ride a bike yet.

CASSANDRA: Really? She's the best runner I know!

ALEX: I'm going to give her my old bike.

CASSANDRA: The little one? Let's teach her how to ride.

ALEX: We can go riding on the field. I'll give her a little push to get her started.

CASSANDRA: I'll let her borrow my helmet and knee pads just in case you push her too hard!

ALEX: I won't push her too hard. Just a little push. She'll be okay. She just needs to learn how to balance.

"A" my name is Adam and I'm riding on macadam.

"P" my name is Pickle and I'm riding my bicycle.

Sand and gravel,
On the road.
Watch out rider,
Don't hit that toad!

"H" my name is Harris and I'm riding straight to Paris.

ALEX CYCLES FOR CHARITY

I am going to cycle in a PMC Kids Ride. The PMC Kids Ride raises money to help find a cure for cancer. PMC stands for Pan-Mass Challenge.

Kids raise $25 dollars to do the ride, but I'm going to try to raise more. I will ask my friends family, and neighbors for donations. Then I'm going to have a bike wash to raise extra money. If you come to my bike wash, you can get a bike washed for $2.00 and be philanthropic at the same time.

STUFF
PMC Kids get T-shirts, parties, and good food.

MY GOALS
1. I want to ride 25 miles.

2. I hope to raise $100.

Phil-an-thro-py is a new word for me. It means giving, helping, kind-ness, and charity. I'll be washing my own bike, too, and when I do, I'm going to donate my own $2.00.

3. Some-day I will ride in the adult PMC. It's a 190-mile ride from Sturbridge, MA to Provincetown, MA. You have to be 15-years old to do the big PMC.

Why am I doing the Kids PMC?
1. Fun: It's always fun to ride my bike.
2. Philanthropy: I can help save lives. I can help people with cancer get better.
3. Charity: The money I raise will be used for research. Research is like an investigation. People do studies to find new treatments for cancer patients.
4. Love: I am doing this ride in honor of my grandmother who has cancer. I'm going to write "Grandma" in a heart and pin it to the back of my shirt.

PMC Kids Rides Web site: https://kids.pmc.org

Bicycle Vocabulary

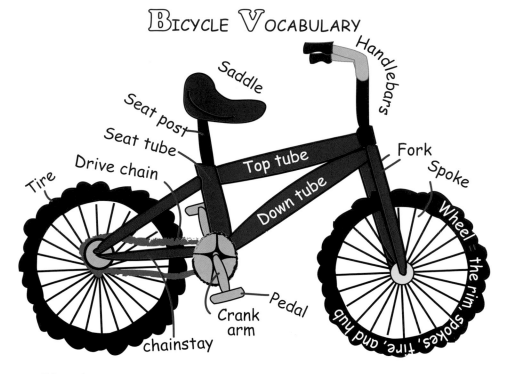

Bicycle - Vehicle with 2 wheels, run by pedal power.

Top tube - Cylinder that connects the seat tube to the head tube.

Drive chain - Set of metal links used to transfer motion.

Fork - Two parallel tubes that hold the front wheel in place.

Saddle - Bicycle seat.

Spoke - Long thin piece of metal that connects the rim of the wheel to the center of the wheel.

Pedal
Power

Riding on the trail,
Hitting every stick,
Jumping over all the rocks,
Going pretty quick!

Like my

bike!

OUTDOOR SAFETY

Running and cycling are outdoor activities. Here are some safety tips.

1. Always exercise with at least one buddy.

2. Dress properly for the weather. Children are more sensitive to hot and cold temperatures than adults.

3. Let your parents know where you are going and what time you will be home.

4. Wear reflective clothing, if there is a chance that it may be getting dark when you are heading home.

5. Wear a helmet if you cycle.

6. Don't use headsets while exercising outdoors. You need to be able to listen to the sounds around you.

7. If someone stops to ask directions, don't get close to their car. Don't talk to strangers.

8. Run against the traffic. Cycle with the traffic. Stop at stop signs. Make sure the drivers see you before crossing the street.

9. Run and cycle with family, friends, clubs, and class.

10. Drink water before and after you run. Drink water while you cycle.

11. Keep your bike in good repair.

12. Exercise in your own neighborhood.

TIPS

Hey, Fastguy, the dogs are "all four" running.

Me, "two".

I'm all for running!!

I'm 4 today!!

The kids have their best run ever after taking some time to cross-train.

Find some good places to run and cycle. Rail trails are areas made for these activities. Ask your parents to plan a vacation near a rail trail. It will be fun to run and ride with the whole family.

State parks often have running and cycling trails. Again, encourage Mom and Dad to go with you.

Enter events and join clubs. This way you'll always have people to exercise with.

Cycling is great on the hotter days.

Activities
Learn the parts of a bike.
Take a day off from running to ride.
Make up some "Blank - my name is blank and I'm riding blank blank blank" poems.

Your run may feel better after you've taken off some time to cycle.

LEARNING TO RIDE A BIKE

Many children learn to ride a bike very easily. They are riding a two-wheeler before they enter school. Others learn when they are 6 or 7 years old. But some children don't learn without difficulty. These tips are for that child, the child who is 8, 9, 10 or older and has never been able to ride a two-wheeler.

First, you need to learn how to balance. Make sure that you are learning on a bike on which your feet can touch the ground. The bike you learn to ride on should be smaller than one you would buy for riding. If you don't own a small bike, borrow one from a younger or smaller friend.

Wear a helmet and cycling gloves. They will protect you if you fall. You can learn on a field, at the park, or in your own driveway.

With this smaller bike, you can practice scooting along by moving your feet and gliding a bit on your bike. Practice without pedaling. Get used to balancing on your bike.

Have a friend or parent give you a push. To do this, they hold onto the bike saddle and give you a gentle push. You can peddle a little and put your feet down to the ground or pavement to brake. Later you can use the bike's brakes.

If you feel awkward with a friend then practice on your own. Use a small bike and scoot along. Have confidence. Once you learn to balance and ride, you will never forget. You'll always be able to ride.

Maybe I'll do the PMC one day, too!

MILE BASICS

The mile is a middle distance often used to test your ability to keep running. The mile test is a measure of speed and endurance.

If you run around a typical high school track 4 times, then you have run a mile. To be able to do this well, you must practice running.

There are different standards for running a mile. A mile standard is a goal that girls and boys of different ages should be able to run.

It's helpful to know how many miles away places are from your home. Knowing distances in miles helps you communicate with others.

I'll be so proud. It'll make me smile, when first I'm able to run a mile.

Run far!

We're singing and running,
Around the high school track.
We're moving and grooving,
While in a friendly pack.

Run easy!

TRAINING SCHEDULE: From Coach Ed

Before you even think about getting faster at running the mile, you need to be able to run the distance at an easy pace.

In training for the mile the emphasis is on endurance or stamina. This means that you can keep going for a long time. Your goal will be to complete the mile run without stopping.

HOW TO GET THERE
Run for 3 minutes without stopping. Keep your pace slow. Once you can do that you can set up a training schedule.

Do that 3-minute run, 3 days a week. The next week of training do a 4-min. run, 3 days a week. Up your runs the following week by 2 minutes, running 6-min. runs, for 3 days. The last week of training do 8-min. runs, for 3 days. Now you are ready to run the mile. Not only will the mile be easy for you, without even knowing it you just got yourself into supershape. This easy 6-week training program will give you the stamina to be a better athlete in any sport you do.

SCHEDULE

Week 1: Adjust your pace so you can **run 3 minutes** without stopping.

Week 2: Do a **3-minute run, 3 days** a week.

Week 3: **4-minute run, 3 days** a week.

Week 4: **6-minute run, 3 days** a week.

Week 5: **8-minute run, 3 days** a week.

Week 6: **Run the mile.**

ALEX: What were you and Karlie doing at recess?

CASSANDRA: We were training for the mile run!

ALEX: But you can already run a mile.

CASSANDRA: I'm going to try to get a little faster.

ALEX: So just what were you guys doing?

CASSANDRA: We walked and then we did some sprints and jogs. Then we walked some more.

ALEX: Want me to time you on a sprint tomorrow?

CASSANDRA: Yes, yes, yes!

"K" my name is Kyle and I'm going to run a mile.

"J" my name is Jack and I'm running 'round the track.

A belly-running crocodile,
Is getting ready to swim.
I'd run a mile the other way,
To get away from him!

"G" my name is Gail and I'm jogging on a trail.

TURNING YOUR TRAINING INTO PLAY

There are a lot of ways that runners turn their training into play. You can do this, too. If you are following Coach Ed's mile schedule 3 days each week, then you can try these on some of the other days.

HILLS make you strong.
1. Find a small grassy hill.
2. Warm up by walking, jogging, doing a few jumping jacks, and skipping.
3. Run up the hill.
4. When you get to top of the hill walk 10 steps away from the hill. Turn around and walk back to the hill.
5. Run down the hill and back up again.
6. Repeat steps 3-5 a few times.
7. Cool down by walking and jogging.

SPRINTS make you fast.
1. Mark off a 15 meter course.
2. Warm up.
3. Walk the course.
4. Jog the course.
5. Sprint the course.
6. Jog the course.
7. Repeat steps 3-6 a few times.
8. Cool down by walking and jogging.

Dog toys make safe & fun relay batons.

RELAYS What fun!
Take a basic relay and instead of just running the course, make it fun. Carry a ball while you jog, dribble a ball with your feet as in soccer or your hands as in basketball. Carry an egg in a spoon or in a hat. Run to the turnaround and skip back. Run to the turnaround, say the ABCs, then gallop back. Blow bubbles as you run. Run to the turnaround. Pick up the jump rope. Jump 10 times and run back. Run to the turnaround. Pick up a hula hoop. Twirl the hula hoop 5 times and run back. Use your imagination to create new games.

Metric Mile - The 1500 meters is a race run in many track meets and in the Olympics. It is 3 3/4 times around a 400-meter track, and because it is almost a mile, it is frequently called the metric mile. Some high school races are 1600 meters (exactly 4 laps of a 400-meter track), and these races are also called metric miles.

Mile - 5280 feet or 1609.344 meters, a little more than 4 times around a 400-meter track.

PHRASES

Go the Extra Mile - to work harder, to do more than necessary. Walk a Mile in My Shoes - to understand what it's like to be me.

Jog awhile,

Just a mile.

Move your feet,

Make some heat.

A FAST RELAY: From Coach Ed

Here is a fun workout. Get some 4x100 meter (m) relay teams on the track or field. A 4x100 m relay means that there are 4 legs (or short distances) and each leg is 100 m.

In this relay, one member of each team stands at the start, the 100 m mark, the 200 m mark, and the 300 m mark.

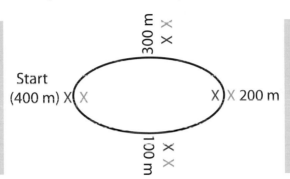

This is how the runners line up before the relay starts.

Diagram shows 8 runners, 2 teams: red team & orange team.

Ready, set, go! The lead-off athletes (athletes at the start) run to the 100 m mark, pass their batons and rest.

The second runners run to the 200 m mark, pass their batons and rest.

The third runners run to the 300 m mark, pass their batons and rest.

The fourth runners run through the 400 m mark (start), then keep going until they get to the 100 m mark. Now they pass their batons. The runners who run from the 300 m mark always run twice as far.

The relay keeps on going! You can play this for a half hour. It's a fun cardio workout that will benefit all types of runners. It will keep your heart pumping and build up your endurance, helping you run faster and farther. In this relay, everyone is a winner.

Running, cycling, walking, and skipping are aerobic exercises.

Running the mile helps you stay fit. As you get fitter, you will be able to run vigorously and still have pep left over for school, homework, and other activities.

Timing the mile is one way to measure cardio endurance. It will tell you how well your lungs and heart carry oxygen and nutrients to your muscles.

Vigorous running helps your body stay lean and your muscles stay strong.

Activities
Walk a mile.
Jog a mile.
Walk and jog a mile.
Jog and run a mile.
Run a mile.

Time yourself.
Set a goal.
Practice.
Try to improve.

KARLIE'S RECESS MILE

I am going to be in the Junior Olympics someday. I love to run and I'm a good runner. Some of my friends run, too. Some of my other friends play soccer.

I'm always in training at recess, but I'm the only one who knows!

I like to play with my friends at recess but I have a secret goal to run at least 1 mile every day. So I wear a pedometer. I play a little soccer. I count the mileage I get while dribbling the soccer ball here and there. Then I jog a lap around our field. I play a at the jump rope station. Then I run another lap. I take a quick walk with a group of girls, and then one more lap. Voila! More than 1 mile. Easy.

When I feel wicked tired I slow down. I walk a little and jog just a bit. I let my body rest and recover. It works. The day after I rest, I seem to run faster and farther than ever and I have a little bounce in my stride.

On those days, I like to bound around part of the field. When I bound, I run for a short time with the longest stride that I can. I look like I'm leaping. I do this for about 10 meters, then I jog a little, then start again. This is skill work. It's a way to become a better runner. Sometimes I do giant skipping. When I do this, the other kids join me and we have fun skipping and laughing.

A 5-K is 5000 meters or 3.1 miles. This is a long distance event.

5-Ks are very popular races. Almost every town has one. Sometimes towns have them to celebrate special days.

When kids run 5-Ks, they usually run as a "finish". Your main goal might be to just cross the finish line.

If you want to run a 5-K, you should be active, learn how to pace yourself, and just do your best. It's helpful to run or run/walk with your family for your first 5-K.

Flat loop. Hot soup. 5-K. Saturday. Flying Crow. We go.

Shoes tied,
TWICE.
Scamper like,
MICE.

5-K SUCCESS

Adult runners love to run 5-Ks. They train for them, keep track of their times, and race often.

Sometimes children want to run 5-Ks and they can. Many run a special once-a-year holiday 5-K with their families. Children usually don't need to follow the same kind of training for 5-Ks as adults. Children are already active with soccer, recess, P.E. class, playing, and some are already kid runners.

If you can answer, "YES!" to the following questions, you should be able to do a 5-K without too much difficulty.

1. Do you play and run for a half hour?

2. Do you often run & walk 1 - 2 miles?

3. Can you control your running so that you can start out at an easy pace, even if it seems like the other runners are going their very fastest?

YOUR PARENTS

If your parents are able, they should help you prepare for your first 5-K. A 5-K for a young runner should be a "finish". A "finish" means that you are participating and not trying to win. It means easy jogging, some kid-sprinting, breaks if needed, and the goal of crossing the finish line.

A 5-K is a long distance race designed for adults not kids, and if your parents are going to run one with you, they should be willing to let you set the pace.

"Take it easy," said my dad. Best advice I ever had.
Next time that I run a race,
I'll trust Dad to set the pace.

ALEX: Doing the Flying Crow 5-K gives us a lot to think about.

CASSANDRA: Yes, kittens, King Kong, & knock-knock jokes. That's a 5-K!

ALEX: You're not TOO silly! Did I tell you that I'm going to run the 5-K with Gage?

CASSANDRA: And I am going to jog the 5-K with Karlie.

ALEX: I've been dreaming about this upcoming 5-K for days and I have come to this conclusion: Kansas City, kickball, knight in shining armor, Key lime pie, & Boy Scout knots.

CASSANDRA: (Giggle) Knitting needles, killer whales, king cobras, kindergarteners, & candy kisses.

(Have fun!)
(Laugh & play.)

Kassie Kitten, on a sunny day,
Got signed up for her first 5-K.
She used her jump rope to quickly train,
And after that, she was never the same.
Knock, knickers, kaboodle, kids, & Kentucky.

THE DAY OF YOUR FIRST 5-K

Get a good night's sleep the night before your first 5-K.
Wake up early. There might be a lot of people going and
your family will need to find a good place to park.

If you have already registered, go to the pre-registration
area. Get your bib-number. **Pin it on the front of your
T-shirt.** You might also get a goody bag and a race
T-shirt. Put these in your car. Runners like to wear their
new tees after their race. They use them to reward them-
selves for crossing the finish line. You can think about
your clean, new, dry T-shirt while you are racing. It's a nice
thought, particularly if it is raining a little during the 5-K.

**If you haven't already paid and registered, you can
often do so on the morning of the event.** You will have to
fill out a form with your name, address, and age. Your
parents will have to sign permission for you to run.

TIME TO RUN

Runners line up before the start of the race. **Don't get in
the front.** The front line is for the fastest adult runners.

Have fun during the race. **Be proud of yourself for doing
a long distance event.** Stay calm. Smile and think good
thoughts. Say things in your head like, *Doing good. Going
easy. I'm cruising. Look at me! I'm SO proud of myself.*

Don't expect a trophy or a medal at the finish line. **Only
the race winners and the age-category winners will get
them.** Sometimes there will be an under-14 or under-12
age category at a 5-K. That is your category. A few boys
and girls, only the very fastest, will get a medal or trophy.

Road-Race Vocabulary

5-K - a 3.1 mile or 5000m distance event.

Age Group - people of the same or similar ages.

Chute - a lane that comes right after the finish line.

Pace - your running or walking speed. Steady speed.

Train - to exercise and eat well while getting ready for an event.

Warm-up - gentle exercise to warm up your muscles.

I run steady.
I am ready.
I run smart.
With a happy heart.

HOLIDAY RACES

What a great way to celebrate a holiday - with a yearly road race! Many people in New England do the Manchester Road Race. This road race is approximately 4.8 miles long - almost 2 miles longer than a 5-K.

I think I'll paint my hand like Tom Turkey when I do the Manchester Road Race. I'll make each finger a different color like a Tom Turkey's tail feathers and I'll add a red wattle and a snood.

Gobble, gobble!

It's been held on Thanksgiving morning for about 70 years. Some people run the race for fun. They dress up in funny costumes and even sing while they run. Some run it to win.

About 10,000 runners attend this race every year.

Amby Burfoot has run this race 45 times. He has also won the race 9 times. That's a record. No one else in the world has won the Manchester Road Race that many times. The first time he ran it, he didn't win the whole race but he won the High School Division. Now that he is older he runs it for fun, but he always tries to do his best. He is more relaxed because he isn't in competition to win the whole race.

Amby eats pasta with sauce the night before the race. He has a bagel and juice for breakfast the morning of the race. After the race he forgets his runner's diet and eats a big turkey dinner with all the trimmings.

I'm cruising.

I need a walking break.

Tips

Get your running clothes ready the night before. Wear the type of clothes and shoes that you trained in.

Eat a good breakfast. Have some cereal, fruit, and drink some water.

Don't get nervous. Remember how you trained. If you walked and ran, then walk and run the 5-K. If you ran easy, then run easy.

Think good thoughts. Tell yourself that you're doing a good job. Be confident and have fun.

208

207

THE FLYING CROW 5-K

Activities
Sign up for a local 5-K.
Train with family and friends.
Think of it as a "finish".
Do this same 5-K every year.
Celebrate running!

Feel the breeze.

THE FLYING CROW 5-K

WHEELCHAIR ATHLETES

Joy entered the Flying Crow 5-K. She is a wheelchair athlete. She has a special sports wheelchair.

She trained with the school running club.

She started with her every-day chair, then got this special sports chair for her birthday.

Joy would get in the front of the pack, because she was faster than the other kids. On club days, one of the parent volunteers would cycle next to Joy to keep her company.

Sometimes she would have a bright flag taped to the back of her chair so that she would be visible. Joy needs special tires to go on the rocky trails. Maybe next year!

COUNTING BY 5s

Ryan Rogers is on the field.
He's working on his upper-body build.
He does 5 crunches,
And then he does 10.
He does 5 more. Here we go again!
How many crunches does Ryan do?
5, 10, 15...

Sometimes Sam does crunches, pushups, and pull-ups to this rhyme. Today he is letting his body recover after the 5-K.

Inspired by an interview with Jean Driscoll, Wheelchair Athlete, 8-time winner, Boston Marathon, author, "Dream Big, Work Hard".

RUNNING-GAME BASICS

Running is child's play especially when it is in the form of a game.

Running games do not have to be competitive. Some running games have winners, others do not. Just as in the fun run, you are a winner if you participate, do your best, and have fun.

The most popular running game is "Tag". There are many forms of tag. It's fun to create your own variety.

Games have rules and the rules should be followed, but if all players agree, it's fun to sometimes change the rules.

Our game is more than a bundle of fun. It's a way to keep us on the run!

Here comes the chicken,
Cluck, cluck, cluck.
If I catch you,
You're a sitting duck!

TAG

There are many versions of the game of tag. Try this one and then make up your own. Have fun, be safe, and run!

DUCKS AND DOGS
1. One boy and one girl are dogs. They stand in the middle of the field barking. They are the taggers or "IT".
2. The rest of the kids are ducks. They stand on the side of the field quacking.
3. One of the dogs yells, "Go," and all the children run. The ducks try to go across the field and back without being tagged. If they are tagged by a dog then they join the dogs in the center of the field and are also "IT".
4. When all the ducks have run across the field and back a dog yells, "Go," again. Play continues like this until all the ducks turn into dogs.
5. Play and have fun! Arf, arf, arf! Quack, quack, quack!
6. Finish with a lap of the field or a hike.

BUTTERFLY TAG
Divide into 2 groups: butterflies (walkers) and netters (runners). The butterflies walk around on the field. The netters run down the running lane, then jog to the field. They tag a walking butterfly. When they tag the butterfly, the butterfly turns into a netter and sprints down the running lane.The netter turns into a butterfly & walks on the field.

Keep playing. It's fun if the walkers carry paper butterflies and give them up to the netters when tagged.

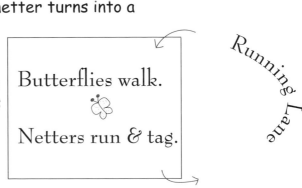

Butterflies walk.

❀

Netters run & tag.

Running Lane

CHITCHAT

ALEX: I could play "Box-stacle Course" every day.

CASSANDRA: Look at me! I'm leaping like an Olympic hurdler.

ALEX: Watch out. Here I come. I'm sprinting to your box!

CASSANDRA: I'm running to the Kangaroo Hop. Hop 10 times, then jog to the next box.

ALEX: This is even more fun than the course we made at school. Let's add some new boxes tomorrow.

A game is a treasure.
You can't measure its pleasure.
It fills you with glee
Pure amusement to me!

"BOX-STACLE COURSES"

Here's a fun game that you will want to play over and over. And it's even more fun if you make it yourself. You will need cardboard boxes, markers, glue, tape, paper, a little imagination AND a lot of energy!

You can play "Box-stacle Course" as a stand-alone game, or you can play it as part of a relay race. In a relay race, the "Box-stacle Course" is the turnaround point. Just run to the boxes, follow the directions, then run back to the start.

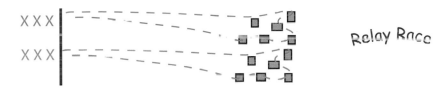

Relay Race

You can also play this as part of a tag game. Get tagged? Do the "Box-stacle Course". And if you make the course interesting enough, everyone will want to get tagged!

SOME "BOX-STACLE" DIRECTIONS
Use these or make up your own. Notice that some of the directions have other everyday equipment like balls and jump ropes.

Leap over, then sprint.	Jump over, then run.
Crawl under, then jog.	Bounce ball 5 times, then run.
Do 4 crunches, then jog.	Do 6 jumping jacks, then walk.
Gallop around, then trot.	Hop around, then leap.
Hurdle, then run.	Jump 'til you miss, then run.
Hop over, then skip.	Do 4 push-ups, then jog.

RUNNING-GAME VOCABULARY

Competition - A contest in which there is a winner whom may be decided by skill, speed, or luck.

Game - Sports play.

Non-competitive - Sports play without a winner or contest.

Rules - A set of guidelines or regulations that you must follow to play fairly.

You yell.
I spell.
What color?
Please tell.

RUN TO SPELL

It's always fun to combine learning with a running game. When you do this, you can practice your skill work and stay healthy and fit at the same time.

RAINBOW SPELLING
You will need crayons, paper, clipboards, and a spelling list. Each player or team has their own clipboard. Clip a piece of paper to it. Ready, set, go! One player calls off a word and a color. Runners pick up that color crayon, run to the paper and write the word, then run back. Play until you have used all the colors of the rainbow.

ONE HUNDRED WORDS
You will need markers, one big numbered chart (1-100) for all of the runners to share, and a short lap course (about 50 meters). Each time a runner completes a lap, he goes to the chart and writes a word (any word), then runs another lap. When the chart is complete, the game is over.

USING MOVEMENT TO LEARN
Sometimes it is fun to use movement to learn to spell difficult words. What is a difficult word? It depends on the speller. Some children find spelling very simple, and others find it hard. Physical activity can make spelling easier. Here are some ideas. Try them and make up your own.

FRIEND: Take 3 sliding steps while you spell, "F-R-I". Then jog in place 3X while you spell, "E-N-D".

HERE, THERE, WHERE: Use a triangle course. Put a box, cone, or sign with the word "HERE" at one corner, a big "T" at another corner, and a "W" at a 3rd corner. Start at "HERE" and shout "H-E-R-E". Run to the "T" and sing, "T-H-E-R-E". Run to the "W" and say, "W-H-E-R-E."

Play running games. You'll run faster and farther when you are having fun without even thinking about it.

Make the games your own. Create themes, signs, and rules. Pretend!

Play both competitive and non-competitive games. Be a well-rounded kid.

Respect the rules. Don't cheat. Play fair. Be a good sport. If you don't like the rules, change them next time you play the game.

Activities

Make a list of your favorite running games.
Invite some friends to play with you.
Include everyone.
Make it fun!

Laugh!

KEEP MOVING

SQUIRRELS, CHIPMUNKS & ACORNS
This is a game that will keep you moving. The object of the game is to collect the most acorns in a certain amount of time. Here is how you play.

Set up the field. You may use any small objects for the "acorns". We use a bucket of colorful plastic math cubes. Scatter the "acorns" around the field. Divide the kids into two teams.

Ready, set, go! Run and find 1 acorn and run back to put it behind your team's start line. Or run across the field to the other team's stash of acorns. Steal one from their stash and carry it back to your team's start line.

RULE: Each squirrel or chipmunk may carry only one acorn at a time. No cheating allowed!

CHIPMUNKS, SQUIRRELS & ACORNS: OTHER VERSIONS

1. Play until one team finds a certain number of acorns. Organize them in groups of 5s or 10s while playing to keep the counting simple.

2. If a runner gets tagged when trying to steal behind the other team's start line, she must give the acorn back.

3. Play for 5 minutes with running. Then play the next 5 minutes with fast walking. Then play the next 5 minutes with running. Keep alternating.

4. Change the theme. In the spring, call the game Robins, Blue Jays & Worms. Use toy plastic creatures.

RUNNING-JOURNAL BASICS

Every runner should have a running journal. A running journal can be used in many different ways.

You can keep track of your runs by telling how far you ran, where you ran, and with whom you ran. You can use it like a diary - a running diary.

Some runners like to be creative with their running journals. They fill them with art, creative writing, and poetry; all inspired by their running.

Others use them like a math or geography journal. They list their times, distances, and map their routes.

Thoughts

If dogs could write,
I think they'd say,
"Take me to school,
On running day."

Ideas

BASIC INFORMATION

You can use a journal to keep track of important information. This information will help you make decisions about your running. Here are some of the most basic things you might want to keep track of. Choose the ones that will be most helpful to you.

Date: Month, date, and year go here.

Distance and Time: Record how far you ran and how long it took you. Are you getting faster? Can you run farther?

Weather: You will find out if you run better in warm or cold weather as well as rainy or dry weather.

Shoes & Clothing: Did you wear your red shoes or blue shoes, your Asics or Nikes?

Running Buddies: Did you run with your dog, friends, classmates, family or team?

Food: Note the foods you ate before you ran.

How You Felt: Did you feel fast, strong, bouncy, tired, or powerful?

Goals: What are your goals for your next run?

Don't forget to leave some room for creativity. Sometimes the rhythm of a run stimulates your brain. Perhaps you thought of a poem while out running or came up with a great idea for a story you'd like to write. Save a spot in your journal for these brainstorms.

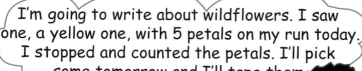

When it's the end of running day, I open my journal and express away.

If I run a trail,
Or take a walk,
I never end up with,
Writers' block.

Reflect

Dream

CASSANDRA'S WRITING PEP TALK

Do you want to be a writer? Do you long to write stories, books, or poetry? If you do, then your running journal is a great place to start. Everyone should get to enjoy running & writing. You'll get better at both with some practice. You may just discover that you are fabulous, awesome, & magnificent!

Here's what you do. **First, you need a journal.** Think of it as a portfolio. A portfolio is a special scrapbook that a writer uses to keep samples of his or her work.

You can buy a writers' journal at the store. I have a gold one that snaps shut. It's like string without any beads. I'm saving it for my very best writing. And once I add words, it will sparkle.

For now, I use my everyday journal. When it was new, it was like an unfrosted gingerbread boy. It was homemade and plain. Now that I'm writing in it, it's coming to life.

You can make your own. Just staple a bunch of pages together. Use different kinds of paper, so that it'll inspire you to try different kinds of writing and drawing, too!

If you have a very small journal, you can take it with you on your runs. Then take notes so that you don't forget your deepest thoughts.

Rule: Don't let anyone discourage you when it comes to running or writing. Show your journal to people who will encourage you! Run, write, & draw.

Running-Journal Vocabulary

Diary - A book in which you write about your experiences.

Journal - A diary, logbook, creative writing notebook, sketchbook, or a scrapbook to keep memories.

Logbook - A book in which you keep a true record of running data: times, weather miles, routes, races.

If a dog were writing, it'd be about lightning.

Alex shares his logbook,
With everyone he knows,
But Cassandra hides her journal,
Under a pile of winter clothes.

Write to share.   *Write for yourself.*

KIDS RUNNING WEB SITES

Here are a few Web sites that will inspire you to run, write, or track your mileage. All Web sites should be viewed with or by your parents.

CAROL GOODROW (carolgoodrow.com)
Author site with fitness/running books, printables, teaching strategies, and more.

FITNESS FINDERS (fitnessfinders.net)
Home of the popular school toe-token mileage program. Kids who participate in a school program earn colorful plastic toe-tokens to tie to their shoes.

IAN'S SHOELACE SITE (fieggen.com/shoelace/)
Learn to tie your shoes, or if you can already tie, try some fancy ways of tying. Artistic kids will love the creative methods.

JUST RUN (justrun.org)
Full of information for any parent or teacher. Justrun.org has many ideas for tracking mileage and lots of fitness info.

KIDS RUNNING (kidsrunning.com)
KidsRunning.com is the original kids' running Web site. You can download free printables for logging mileage. You can also find a list of model kids running programs across the nation.
Model programs: http://www.kidsrunning.com/krlinks
This Web site is affiliated with Runner's World magazine.

PE CENTRAL (pecentral.org)
PE Central is a teacher site. It has a Log It program. You can log your steps or miles as you virtually walk or run across America.
Log It program: http://www.peclogit.org/logit.asp

USTAF (usatf.org)
If you want to be in the Junior Olympics, then start here. Look for a USATF affiliated club or team to join. Visit the youth section.

Joining a team will give you plenty to write about!

Make exercise part of everything you do. Read, write, and dream about running.

Save your completed running journal. Put it in a treasure chest, keep it in your drawer, and look back at it. It will inspire you to keep running. Read it to remember the fantastic times you have had.

And when your journal is complete, start another. Keep running, have fun, and enjoy a lifetime of fitness.

Activities

Make a list of all the healthy foods you eat during the week.
Write about your favorite places to run.
Keep track of your mileage until you have run a marathon (26.2).
Once a month, time yourself on a short route. Write your times in your journal.
How long are you exercising every day? Keep track in your journal.

KIDS RUNNING BOOKS

Reading and writing go hand-in-hand. Here are some books that will inspire you to run. While you read, think about what the author has to say. Make a connection to your own running. Then express your thoughts in your journal.

CHAPTER BOOK
The Treasure of Health and Happiness by Carol Goodrow

JOURNAL
Happy Feet, Healthy Food: Your Child's First Journal of Exercise & Healthy Eating by Carol Goodrow

CHILDREN'S PICTURE BOOKS
Myrtle the Hurdler and her Pink and Purple, Polka-Dotted Girdle by Marybeth Dillon-Butler, illustrated by David Messing

CoCo Loves to Tri by Michele Bredice Craemer, illustrated by Jess Golden

Pellie Runs a Marathon by Michele Bredice Craemer, illustrated by Elizabeth Lavin

See Mom Run by Kara Douglass Thom, illustrated by Lilly Golden

Slow Days, Fast Friends by Erik Brooks

We Are Girls Who Love to Run by Brianna Grant, illustrated by Nicholas A. Wright

Run, Dogs, Run! by Hal Higdon, illustrated by Dana Summers

INSPIRATION
Girls Lit from Within, A Guide to Life Outside of the Girl Box by Molly Barker

Jean Driscoll: Dream Big, Work Hard! by Michael Sandler and Jean Driscoll

PARENTS AND TEACHERS
Fit Kids, Smarter Kids by Jeff Galloway

TRACK

If you want to be in the Junior Olympics, then you might
join a track team. With the help of a coach, you can find an
event that is just right for you, like the 100, 200, 400, 800,
1500, and 3000 meters. Or perhaps you'd like to run a
relay. You can choose a 4x100 or a 4x400 meter relay. And
there is more. If you run indoor
track, you can run 50, 300, 600, and
1000 meters.

Do you like to jump? Then you could
have fun with the hurdles, long
jump or high jump.

And don't forget the field events:
Shot put - Throw a heavy ball.
Javelin - Throw a light spear or Turbo Jav (plastic javelin).
Discus - Throw a heavy disk.

Thank you to Coach Ed Poirier for help with this section.

Here's what you do. Visit usatf.org. Look for their youth
section. Read about the Junior Olympics. Then find a club
through their Web site. It will be easier to be involved in
the Junior Olympics if you are part of a team.   On a team,
you will practice, try different events, and compete in one
of many age divisions.

Division	Your Age on December 31 of the Year
Bantam	10-and-under
Midget	11-12
Youth	13-14
Intermediate	15-16
Young Men/Women	17-18*

* With the condition that a recent high school graduate
may compete in the track & field program if they do not
turn 19 by the end of the nationals.

CROSS-COUNTRY RUNNING

Cross-country running can be abbreviated as XC.

If you love to run on the trails, up and down hills, over rocks and roots, in the woods, across winding paths, then cross-country running may be the sport for you.

You can run cross-country for a team, at an event, or with your dog. If you love to compete then you can run XC in the Junior Olympics. Competitive cross-country distances are from 3K - 5K. This is long distance running, so you will need to build up your endurance.

Cross-country routes are varied and unique. They are full of wonderful treats such as babbling brooks and waterfalls.

Autumn is a popular time to run cross-country. The weather is cool, the leaves are turning beautiful colors, and the trails are fairly dry. But somedays the trails will be wet, so you can't worry about getting muddy if you are a cross-country runner.

The terrain or ground of cross-country running will vary more than the surface of a track or road, but you will develop strong ankles and be treated to the changes of seasons as a cross-country runner and you will see sights you would not see elsewhere. You might see a family of deer, a great blue heron, a beaver, a pileated woodpecker, a weasel, or a rabbit. Cross-country running will give you memories to last for a lifetime.

OTHER BOOKS BY CAROL GOODROW

Available in bookstores everywhere.
www.breakawaybooks.com